MW01178147

TREATS

just great recipes

GENERAL INFORMATION

The level of difficulty of the recipes in this book
is expressed as a number from 1 (simple) to 3 (difficult).

TREATS
just great recipes

focaccia

McRae Books

MAKES one (12-inch/30-cm) focaccia
PREPARATION 20 min
RISING TIME 1 h 30 min
COOKING 20–25 min
DIFFICULTY level 1

Basic Focaccia

Prepare the yeast as shown on page 5. • Prepare the dough as shown below. • Preheat the oven to 425°F (220°C/gas 7). • When the rising time has elapsed (about 1 hour 30 minutes), transfer the dough to a lightly floured work surface and knead for 2–3 minutes. • Place the dough on an oiled baking sheet and, using your hands, spread into a disk about 12 inches (30 cm) in diameter and 1/2 inch (1 cm) thick. Dimple the surface with your fingertips. Drizzle with the remaining oil and sprinkle with the coarse sea salt, if using (salt is good for plain focaccia; it may clash with other toppings). • Bake until pale golden brown, 20–25 minutes.

1 oz (30 g) fresh yeast or 2 (1/4-oz/7-g) packages active dry yeast
1 teaspoon sugar
About 3/4 cup (200 ml) warm water
3 1/3 cups (500 g) all-purpose (plain) flour
1 teaspoon fine salt
1/4 cup (60 ml) extra-virgin olive oil
1 tablespoon coarse sea salt (optional)

The dough

1 Sift the flour and salt into a large bowl. Pour in the yeast mixture, most of the remaining water, and any other ingredients listed in the recipe. Stir until the flour is absorbed, adding more water as required.

2 Sprinkle a work surface with a little flour (note that flour used

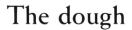

The yeast

To prepare the yeast you will need a small bowl, a fork, warm water, and sugar. Exact quantities are given in each recipe.

1 Put the fresh or active dry yeast in the bowl. If using fresh yeast, crumble it into the bowl.

2 Add the sugar and half the warm water and stir with a fork

until the yeast has dissolved.

3 Set the mixture aside for about 10 minutes. It will look creamy when ready. Stir again before proceeding to make the dough.

to prepare the work surface is not included in the quantities given in the recipes. Allow about $^1/_2$ cup/75 g extra). Transfer the dough to the work surface. Shape into a compact ball.

3 Press down on the dough with your knuckles to spread it. Take the far end of the dough, fold it a short distance toward you, then push it away again with

the heel of your palm. Flexing your wrist, fold it toward you again, give it a quarter turn, then push it away. Repeat, gently and with the lightest possible touch, for 8–10 minutes. When ready, the dough should be smooth and elastic, show definite air bubbles beneath the surface, and spring back if you flatten it with your palm.

4 Place in a large bowl and cover with a cloth. It should double in volume during rising. To test, poke your finger gently into the dough; if the impression remains, it is ready. The rising times given are approximate; yeast is a living ingredient affected by temperature and humidity, among other things. Some days it will take longer to rise than others.

SERVES 4–6
PREPARATION 25 min
RISING TIME 2 h 30 min
COOKING 35–40 min
DIFFICULTY level 2

Potato Focaccia
with cherry tomatoes and oregano

Cook the potato in a small pot of salted boiling water until tender, about 10 minutes. Drain and mash until smooth. • Prepare the focaccia dough following the instructions on pages 4–5. Gradually work the mashed potato into the dough as you knead. Let rise in a warm place until doubled in volume, about 2 hours. • Oil a 10-inch (25-cm) baking pan and press the dough into it using your fingers. Sprinkle with the tomatoes, coarse salt, and oregano. • Drizzle with the remaining oil and let rise for 30 minutes. • Preheat the oven to 425°F (220°C/gas 7). • Bake until the focaccia is golden brown, 25–30 minutes. • Serve hot or at room temperature.

1 large floury (baking) potato, peeled and cut into small cubes
1 lb (500 g) basic focaccia dough (see pages 4–5)
2 tablespoons extra-virgin olive oil
20 cherry tomatoes, halved
1 teaspoon coarse salt
1 tablespoon finely chopped oregano

SERVES 4-6
PREPARATION 35 min
RISING TIME 1 h 30 min
COOKING 20–25 min
DIFFICULTY level 1

Focaccia
with onion and bacon

Prepare the focaccia dough following the instructions on pages 4–5. Let rise in a warm place until doubled in volume. • Preheat the oven to 400°F (200°C/gas 6). • Oil a large baking sheet. • Turn the dough out onto a lightly floured work surface and knead for 5 minutes. • Roll out into a ½-inch (1-cm) thick disk. • Place the dough on the prepared baking sheet and fold the edges in, pinching to make a border. Prick with a fork. • Cover with the cheese, onion, bacon, and potato. Sprinkle with the thyme, season with salt, and drizzle with the oil. • Bake until the focaccia is golden brown, 20–25 minutes. • Serve hot or at room temperature.

1 lb (500 g) basic focaccia dough (see pages 4–5)
8 oz (250 g) Crescenza or other soft fresh cheese, cut into small pieces
1 small onion, finely sliced
3 oz (90 g) bacon, chopped
2 small waxy potatoes, peeled and very thinly sliced
1 tablespoon finely chopped thyme
2 tablespoons extra-virgin olive oil

SERVES 4–6

PREPARATION 25 min

RISING TIME 2 h

COOKING 15–20 min

DIFFICULTY level 1

Focaccia

with extra-virgin olive oil

Prepare the focaccia dough following the instructions on pages 4–5. Gradually work 4 tablespoons of the oil into the dough as you knead. Let rise in a warm place until doubled in volume, about 2 hours. • Preheat the oven to 425°F (220°C/gas 7). • Oil two baking sheets. • Turn the dough out onto a lightly floured work surface and knead for 5 minutes. • Divide the dough into two equal portions. Roll out each piece of dough on a lightly floured work surface to make a 12 inch (30 cm) disk. • Transfer the dough to the prepared baking sheets and fold in the edges, pinching slightly to make a border. Sprinkle with the coarse sea salt and drizzle with the remaining oil. • Bake until the focaccia is golden brown, 15–20 minutes. • Serve hot or at room temperature.

1 lb (500 g) basic focaccia dough
(see pages 4–5)
½ cup (125 ml) extra-virgin olive oil
1 tablespoon coarse sea salt

Baby Focaccias
with tomato and prosciutto

Prepare the focaccia dough following the instructions on pages 4–5. • Divide the dough into walnut-size balls and place, well-spaced, on a lightly floured work surface. Cover with a cloth and let rise until doubled in size, about 1 hour. • Preheat the oven to 375°F (190°C/gas 5). • Oil two baking sheets. • Roll out each ball of dough to make a disk about 4 inches (10 cm) in diameter. • Arrange the disks on the prepared baking sheets. • Bake until golden brown, 12–15 minutes. • While the focaccias are in the oven, heat 1 tablespoon of the remaining oil in a small frying pan over medium heat. Add the prosciutto, onion, and capers and sauté until the onion is tender, about 5 minutes. • Add the tomatoes, parsley, and basil. Simmer until the tomato begins to break down, about 5 minutes. • Stir in the remaining oil. • Place the hot focaccias on a serving dish and spread each one with a little of the sauce. • Serve hot.

1 lb (500 g) basic focaccia dough (see pages 4–5)
3 tablespoons extra-virgin olive oil
4 oz (125 g) sliced prosciutto (Parma ham), cut into ribbons
1 small onion, finely sliced
1 tablespoon salt-cured capers, rinsed and coarsely chopped
3 medium tomatoes, peeled and chopped
2 tablespoons finely chopped parsley
2 tablespoons finely chopped basil

SERVES 4–6

PREPARATION 25 min

RISING TIME 2 h 30 min

COOKING 25–30 min

DIFFICULTY level 1

Focaccia
with olive pâté

Prepare the focaccia dough following the instructions on pages 4–5. • Oil a 10-inch (25-cm) pizza or quiche pan. • Turn the dough out onto a lightly floured work surface and knead for 5 minutes. • Press into the prepared pan using your fingers. • Spread with the olive pâté. Sprinkle with the olives and drizzle with the remaining oil. • Cover with a cloth and let rise for 1 hour in a warm place. • Preheat the oven to 425°F (220°C/gas 7). Sprinkle the focaccia with oregano. • Bake until golden brown, 25–30 minutes. • Serve hot or at room temperature.

1 lb (500 g) basic focaccia dough (see pages 4–5)

2 tablespoons extra-virgin olive oil

5 oz (150 g) black olive pâté

1½ cups (150 g) pitted black olives, quartered

1 teaspoon dried oregano

SERVES 4–6
PREPARATION 30 min
RISING TIME 2 h
COOKING 20–25 min
DIFFICULTY level 2

Focaccia
with cherry tomatoes and basil

Prepare the focaccia dough following the instructions on pages 4–5. Gradually work 2 tablespoons of the oil into the dough as you knead. Let rise in a warm place until doubled in volume, about 2 hours. • Preheat the oven to 450°F (250°C/gas 8). • Oil a 12-inch (30-cm) pizza or quiche pan. • Turn the dough out onto a lightly floured work surface and knead for 5 minutes. • Press the dough into the prepared pan using your fingers. • Cover with the tomatoes. Season with salt and pepper. Drizzle with the remaining oil. • Bake until the focaccia is golden brown, 20–25 minutes. • Garnish with the basil. Serve hot or at room temperature.

1 lb (500 g) basic focaccia dough (see pages 4–5)
1/4 cup (60 ml) extra-virgin olive oil
12–16 cherry tomatoes, sliced
Salt and freshly ground black pepper
Fresh basil, to garnish

Spicy Focaccia

Dissolve the yeast in the milk in a small bowl. • Sift the flour into a large bowl. Stir in the polenta and salt. • Add the eggs, butter, yeast mixture, and chile pepper. Stir well with a wooden spoon to make a soft dough. • Transfer to a lightly floured work surface and knead until smooth and elastic, 5–10 minutes. • Place the dough in an oiled bowl and cover with a clean cloth. Let rise in a warm place for 1 hour. • Preheat the oven to 375°F (190°C/gas 5). • Oil a 10-inch (25-cm) pizza or quiche pan using your fingers. • Bake until the focaccia is golden brown, 25–30 minutes. • Serve hot or at room temperature.

- ½ oz (15 g) fresh yeast or 1 (¼-oz/7-g) package active dry yeast
- ⅓ cup (90 ml) milk, warmed
- 1 cup (150 g) all-purpose (plain) flour
- 1 cup (150 g) fine polenta (stoneground cornmeal)
- ½ teaspoon salt
- 3 large eggs, lightly beaten
- ⅔ cup (150 g) butter, melted
- 1 red chile pepper, seeded and finely chopped

Filled Focaccia

with goat cheese

Sift the flour into a large bowl. Add half the oil and the water. Mix to make a smooth dough. Shape into a ball and wrap in plastic wrap (cling film). • Chill in the refrigerator for 1 hour. • Put the goat cheese in a small bowl and stir until smooth. • Add half the thyme and season with salt and pepper. • Preheat the oven to 400°F (200°C/gas 6). • Oil a large baking sheet. • Divide the dough into 8 pieces. Roll out on a lightly floured work surface into $1/8$-inch (3-mm) thick ovals. • Spread half the dough with the cheese mixture, leaving a $3/4$-inch (2-cm) border around the edges. • Beat the egg white and water in a small bowl. Brush the edges of the pastry with this mixture. • Cover the filled focaccias with the remaining dough. Pinch the edges together to seal. • Place on the prepared sheet. Brush with some of the remaining oil. • Bake for 5 minutes. Brush with the remaining oil. • Bake until puffed and golden brown, 5–10 minutes. • Serve hot.

$1^2/_3$ cups (250 g) all-purpose (plain) flour
$1/_3$ cup (90 ml) extra-virgin olive oil
$1/_3$ cup (90 ml) water
5 oz (150 g) soft goat cheese
2 tablespoons finely chopped thyme
Salt and freshly ground black pepper
1 large egg white
2 tablespoons water

Focaccia

with ham, cheese, and tomatoes

Prepare the focaccia dough following the instructions on pages 4–5. Gradually work 2 tablespoons of the oil into the dough as you knead. Let rise in a warm place until doubled in volume, about 2 hours. • Preheat the oven to 425°F (220°C/gas 7). • Oil a 12-inch (30-cm) pizza or quiche pan. • Turn the dough out onto a lightly floured work surface and knead for 5 minutes. • Press the dough into the prepared pan using your fingers. • Season with salt and drizzle with the remaining oil. • Bake until the focaccia is golden brown, 20–25 minutes. • Top with the mozzarella, ham, tomatoes, and olives. Sprinkle with chile pepper, if liked. • Serve warm.

1 lb (500 g) basic focaccia dough (see pages 4–5)

1/4 cup (60 ml) extra-virgin olive oil

4 oz (125 g) fresh mozzarella cheese, drained and thinly sliced

5 oz (150 g) ham, sliced

5 oz (150 g) cherry tomatoes, halved

1/2 cup (50 g) pitted green olives

1 red chile pepper, seeded and sliced (optional)

SERVES 4–6
PREPARATION 30 min
RISING TIME 2 h
COOKING 20–25 min
DIFFICULTY level 2

Herb Focaccia

Prepare the focaccia dough following the instructions on pages 4–5. Gradually work 2 tablespoons of the oil into the dough as you knead. Let rise in a warm place until doubled in volume, about 2 hours. • Preheat the oven to 450°F (250°C/gas 8). • Turn the dough out onto a lightly floured work surface and knead for 5 minutes. Press the dough into an oiled 8 x12-inch (20 x 30-cm) baking pan using your fingers. • Mix together the onion, garlic, parsley, basil, rosemary, and oregano in a small bowl. Add 2 tablespoons of the remaining oil and season with pepper. Spread the tomatoes over the focaccia and top with the herb mixture. Season with salt and drizzle with the remaining oil. • Bake until the focaccia is golden brown, 20–25 minutes. • Serve hot or at room temperature.

1 lb (500 g) basic focaccia dough (see pages 4–5)
1/3 cup (90 ml) extra-virgin olive oil
1 medium onion, very finely chopped
2 cloves garlic, very finely chopped
3 tablespoons finely chopped parsley
2 tablespoons finely chopped basil
1 tablespoon finely chopped rosemary
1/2 teaspoon dried oregano
Salt and freshly ground black pepper
1 (14-oz/400-g) can tomatoes, with juice, chopped

SERVES 4–6

PREPARATION 15 min

COOKING 50 min

DIFFICULTY level 1

Easy Focaccia
with zucchini

Heat 3 tablespoons of the oil in a large frying pan over medium heat. Add the onion and water. Sauté until the onion is tender, about 5 minutes. Season with salt and pepper. • Preheat the oven to 350°F (180°C/gas 4). • Oil a 10-inch (25-cm) springform pan. • Sift the flour and baking powder into a large bowl. Add the milk, remaining oil, eggs, zucchini, and onion. Season with salt and pepper and mix well. • Spoon the mixture into the prepared pan. • Bake until golden brown and a skewer inserted into the center comes out clean, about 50 minutes. • Serve hot or at room temperature.

⅓ cup (90 ml) extra-virgin olive oil
1 medium white onion, finely sliced
2 tablespoons water
Salt and freshly ground black pepper
2 cups (300 g) all-purpose (plain) flour
2 teaspoons baking powder
⅓ cup (90 ml) milk
3 large eggs, lightly beaten
4 zucchini (courgettes), cut into tiny cubes

Garlic Focaccia
with mortadella and cheese

Cook the potatoes in a small pot of salted boiling water until tender, about 10 minutes. Drain and mash until smooth. • Prepare the focaccia dough following the instructions on pages 4–5. Gradually work the potato and 1 tablespoon of oil into the dough as you knead. Let rise in a warm place until doubled in volume, about 2 hours. • Preheat the oven to 400°F (200°C/gas 6). • Turn the dough out onto a lightly floured work surface and knead for 5 minutes. • Oil a 12-inch (30-cm) pizza or quiche pan and press the dough into it using your fingers. • Sprinkle with the garlic. Top with the tomatoes. Sprinkle with salt and oregano. Drizzle with the remaining oil. • Bake until golden brown, 20–25 minutes. • Top with mortadella and cheese and serve hot or at room temperature.

2 large floury (baking) potatoes, peeled and cut into small cubes

1 lb (500 g) basic focaccia dough (see pages 4–5)

1/4 cup (60 ml) extra-virgin olive oil

4 cloves garlic, halved

12 cherry tomatoes, sliced

1 teaspoon dried oregano

4 oz (125 g) mortadella or ham, sliced

4 oz (125 g) Provolone or other firm mature cheese, thinly sliced

SERVES 4–6
PREPARATION 45 min
RISING TIME 2 h
COOKING 30–35 min
DIFFICULTY level 2

Filled Focaccia
with onion and olives

Prepare the focaccia dough following the instructions on pages 4–5. • Oil a baking sheet. • Turn the dough out onto a lightly floured work surface and knead for 5 minutes. • Roll it out into a large oval about ½-inch (1-cm) thick. • Mix together the onions, olives, and ½ tablespoon of rosemary in a medium bowl. • Add 2 tablespoons of oil and a pinch of salt. Mix well. • Spoon the mixture over half the dough, leaving ¾ inch (2 cm) free around the edges. • Brush the edges with water and then fold the remaining dough over the filling. Press the edges together to seal. • Sprinkle with the sea salt and remaining rosemary. Brush with the remaining oil. Let rise for 30 minutes. • Preheat the oven to 350°F (180°C/gas 4). • Bake until risen and golden brown, 30–35 minutes. • Serve hot or at room temperature.

1½ lb (750 g) basic focaccia dough (see pages 4–5)
¼ cup (60 ml) extra-virgin olive oil
3 large sweet red onions, finely sliced
Salt
1½ cups (150 g) pitted black olives, coarsely chopped
1 tablespoon finely chopped rosemary

SERVES 4–6
PREPARATION 30 min
RISING TIME 2 h 45 min
COOKING 35–40 min
DIFFICULTY level 2

Filled Focaccia
with zucchini and tomatoes

Prepare the focaccia dough following the instructions on pages 4–5. Gradually work the oil, lard, and 1 tablespoon of rosemary into the dough as you knead. Let rise in a warm place until doubled in volume, about 2 hours. • Preheat a grill pan or griddle over medium heat. Grill the zucchini on both sides until tender and lightly browned. • Oil an 8-inch (20-cm) square baking pan. • Divide the dough into 2 equal portions. Press half the dough into the base and sides of the prepared pan. • Cover with the mozzarella and zucchini. Season with salt and pepper. • Roll out the remaining dough on a lightly floured work surface until it is large enough to cover the pan. Press the edges together to seal. Prick the dough with a fork. Let rise for 45 minutes. • Preheat the oven to 425°F (220°C/gas 7). • Brush the focaccia with the remaining oil. Place the tomatoes on top of the focaccia. Sprinkle with the remaining rosemary and season with salt • Bake until the focaccia is golden brown, 25–30 minutes. • Serve hot.

1 lb (500 g) basic focaccia dough (see pages 4–5)
2 tablespoons extra-virgin olive oil
2 tablespoons lard, melted
2 tablespoons fresh rosemary leaves
3 medium zucchini (courgettes), sliced thinly lengthwise
8 oz (250 g) fresh mozzarella cheese, drained and cut into small cubes
Salt and freshly ground black pepper
1–2 tomatoes, thinly sliced

SERVES 4–6
PREPARATION 30 min
RISING TIME 1 h 30 min
COOKING 10 min
DIFFICULTY level 2

Spirals
with cheese and tomato

Dissolve the yeast and sugar in half the milk in a small bowl. • Sift the flour and salt into a large bowl. Add the butter, yeast mixture, mozzarella, and enough milk to make a soft dough. • Transfer to a lightly floured work surface and knead until smooth and elastic, 5–10 minutes. • Shape into a ball and place in an oiled bowl. Cover with a clean cloth and let rise for 30 minutes. • Turn the dough out onto a lightly floured piece of waxed paper. Roll out into a rectangle about 1/8 inch (3 mm) thick. • Spread with the tomato paste. Sprinkle with oregano and Parmesan. • Roll up the dough using the waxed paper to help you. Wrap the roll of dough in the paper and chill in the refrigerator for 15 minutes. • Preheat the oven to 400°F (200°C/gas 6). • Line a baking sheet with waxed paper. • Unwrap the dough and use a sharp knife to slice into 2/3-inch (1.5-cm) slices. Place on the baking sheet and let rise for 1 hour. • Bake until golden brown, about 10 minutes. • Serve hot or at room temperature.

1/2 oz (15 g) fresh yeast or 1 (1/4-oz/ 7-g) package active dry yeast
1 teaspoon sugar
About 1/3 cup (100 ml) milk
2 cups (300 g) all-purpose (plain) flour
1 teaspoon salt
1 oz (30 g) butter, melted
4 oz (125 g) fresh mozzarella cheese, drained and finely chopped
2 oz (60 g) tomato paste (concentrate)
1 teaspoon dried oregano
1/2 cup (60 g) freshly grated Parmesan

SERVES 4–6
PREPARATION 35 min
RISING TIME 2 h
COOKING 20–25 min
DIFFICULTY level 2

Hearty Focaccia
with sausage

Prepare the focaccia dough following the instructions on pages 4–5. Gradually work 2 tablespoons of the oil into the dough as you knead. Let rise in a warm place until doubled in volume, about 2 hours. • Preheat the oven to 425°F (220°C/gas 7). • Oil a 12-inch (30-cm) pizza or quiche pan. • Turn the dough out onto a lightly floured work surface and knead for 5 minutes. Press the dough into the prepared pan using your fingers. • Spread with the ricotta. Top with the eggs and sausage. Sprinkle with olives, oregano, and chile pepper. Season with salt and drizzle with the remaining oil. • Bake until golden brown, 20–25 minutes. • Serve hot or at room temperature.

1 lb (500 g) basic focaccia dough (see pages 4–5)
1/4 cup (60 ml) extra-virgin olive oil
4 boiled eggs, shelled and sliced
6 oz (180 g) ricotta cheese, drained
8 oz (250 g) Italian sausages, skinned and broken into bite-size pieces
10 green olives, pitted and coarsely chopped
1 tablespoon finely chopped oregano
1/2 teaspoon red pepper flakes or crumbled dry chile peppers

SERVES 4–6
PREPARATION 35 min
RISING TIME 2 h
COOKING 30–35 min
DIFFICULTY level 2

Filled Focaccia
with onion

Prepare the focaccia dough following the instructions on pages 4–5. Let rise in a warm place until doubled in volume, about 2 hours. • Preheat the oven to 425°F (220°C/gas 7). • Oil a 12-inch (30-cm) pizza or quiche pan. • Heat the oil in a large frying pan over medium heat. Add the onions and sauté until tender, about 10 minutes. Season lightly with salt. • Turn the dough out onto a lightly floured work surface and knead for 5 minutes. Divide into 2 equal portions. • Roll out each piece of dough into a 12-inch (30-cm) disk. • Line the prepared pan with one of the pieces of dough. • Spread with the onions. Cover with the remaining dough. • Bake until golden brown, 20–25 minutes. • Serve hot or at room temperature.

1 lb (500 g) basic focaccia dough (see pages 4–5)
1/4 cup (60 ml) extra-virgin olive oil
4 large white onions, finely sliced
Salt

SERVES 4–6
PREPARATION 35 min
RISING TIME 3 h 30 min
COOKING 1 h
DIFFICULTY level 3

Potato Focaccia
with cheese and sausage

Cook the potatoes in a large pot of salted boiling until tender, 10–15 minutes. Drain and mash. • Prepare the focaccia dough following the instructions on pages 4–5. Gradually work the potatoes, eggs and 2 tablespoons of the oil into the dough as you knead. Let rise in a warm place until doubled in volume, about 3 hours. • Oil a 12-inch (30-cm) pizza or quiche pan. • Roll out two-thirds of the dough on a lightly floured work surface until large enough to line the prepared pan. Line the pan with the dough. • Cover with the sausage, mozzarella, Emmenthal, and Pecorino. • Roll out the remaining dough and cut into ¾-inch (2-cm) strips using a pastry wheel. Arrange the strips over the focaccia in a lattice pattern. Brush with the remaining oil and sprinkle with the oregano. • Let rise for 30 minutes. • Preheat the oven to 400°F (200°C/gas 6). Bake until the focaccia is golden brown, 35–40 minutes. • Serve hot or at room temperature.

2 medium floury (baking) potatoes, peeled and cut into chunks
1 lb (500 g) basic focaccia dough (see pages 4–5)
2 large eggs
¼ cup (60 ml) extra-virgin olive oil
Salt
3 Italian sausages, skinned and broken into bite-size pieces
5 oz (150 g) mozzarella cheese, cut into small cubes
10 oz (300 g) Emmenthal, coarsely grated
3 tablespoons freshly grated Pecorino cheese
1 teaspoon dried oregano

SERVES 4–6

PREPARATION 30 min

RISING TIME 2 h

COOKING 40 min

DIFFICULTY level 1

Focaccia

with tuna and olives

Prepare the focaccia dough following the instructions on pages 4–5. Gradually work 3 tablespoons of the oil into the dough as you knead. Let rise in a warm place until doubled in volume, about 2 hours. • Heat 2 tablespoons of the remaining oil in a large frying pan over medium heat. Add the onions and sauté until transparent, 3–4 minutes. • Add the olives and sauté for 5 minutes. Season with salt and remove from the heat. Stir in the tuna. • Preheat the oven to 425°F (220°C/gas 7). Oil a 12-inch (30-cm) pizza or quiche pan. • Turn the dough out onto a lightly floured work surface and knead for 5 minutes. • Press two-thirds of the dough into the prepared pan using your fingers. • Spread with the tuna mixture and top with the mozzarella. • Roll out the remaining dough until large enough to cover the pan. Cover the filling with the dough, sealing the edges. Brush with the remaining oil. • Bake until golden brown, about 30 minutes. • Serve hot.

1 lb (500 g) basic focaccia dough (see pages 4–5)

1/3 cup (90 ml) extra-virgin olive oil

2 large onions, finely sliced

1 1/2 cups (150 g) black olives, pitted and coarsely chopped

Salt

6 oz (180 g) tuna preserved in oil, drained and crumbled

4 oz (125 g) fresh mozzarella cheese, drained and cut into small cubes

Baby Focaccias
with salami, beans, and cheese

SERVES 4–6
PREPARATION 35 min
RISING TIME 2 h 30 min
COOKING 25–30 min
DIFFICULTY level 2

Use the first 5 ingredients to prepare the focaccia dough following the instructions on pages 4–5. Cover and let rise until doubled in volume, about 2 hours. • Cook the beans in a large pot of boiling water until tender, about 5 minutes. Drain well. • Oil a baking sheet. • Place the dough on a lightly floured work surface and knead, gradually adding the beans, cheese, salami, and butter as you work. • Divide the dough into egg-size balls. Arrange on the prepared baking sheet, leaving plenty of space between each ball. Let rise for 30 minutes. • Preheat the oven to 350°F (180°C/gas 4). • Brush the baby focaccias with the extra milk. • Bake until risen and golden brown, 20–25 minutes. • Serve hot or at room temperature.

1 oz (30 g) fresh yeast or 2 (¼-oz/7-g) packages active dry yeast
¼ cup (50 g) sugar
¾ cup (200 ml) lukewarm milk + extra, to brush
3⅓ cups (500 g) all-purpose (plain) flour
Salt
4 oz (125 g) fresh or frozen fava (broad) beans
⅓ cup (50 g) coarsely grated Fontina or Cheddar cheese
2 oz (60 g) salami, diced
½ cup (125 g) butter, cut into pieces
1 large egg, lightly beaten

33

SERVES 4–6
PREPARATION 30 min
RISING TIME 2 h 30 min
COOKING 25–30 min
DIFFICULTY level 2

Aromatic Focaccia
with ham and olives

Prepare the focaccia dough following the instructions on pages 4–5. Gradually work 2 tablespoons of the oil into the dough as you knead. Let rise in a warm place until doubled in volume, about 2 hours. • Turn the dough out onto a lightly floured work surface and knead for 5–10 minutes, incorporating the ham, onion, sage, rosemary, and thyme as you work. • Oil a 12-inch (30-cm) pizza or quiche pan. • Press the dough into the prepared pan using your fingers. • Let rise for 30 minutes. • Preheat the oven to 400°F (200°C/gas 6). • Top the focaccia with the olives, pressing them into the dough. Drizzle with the remaining oil and sprinkle with the coarse sea salt. • Bake until the focaccia is risen and golden brown, 25–30 minutes. • Serve hot or at room temperature.

1 lb (500 g) basic focaccia dough
(see pages 4–5)
¼ cup (60 ml) extra-virgin olive oil
4 oz (125 g) ham, very finely chopped
1 small onion, very finely chopped
4 sage leaves, very finely chopped
1 tablespoon finely chopped rosemary
1 tablespoon finely chopped thyme
12 green olives
1 tablespoon coarse sea salt

SERVES 4–6
PREPARATION 25 min
RISING TIME 2 h 30 min
COOKING 25–30 min
DIFFICULTY level 1

Focaccia
with sage and black olives

Prepare the focaccia dough following the instructions on pages 4–5.
• Oil a 12-inch (30-cm) pizza or quiche pan. • Press the dough into the pan with your fingers. Cover and let prove for 30 minutes. • Preheat the oven to 400°F (200°C/gas 6). Brush the focaccia with the oil and sprinkle with the coarse sea salt. • Bake until risen and golden brown, 25–30 minutes. • Serve hot or at room temperature.

1 lb (500 g) basic focaccia dough (see pages 4–5)

2 tablespoons extra-virgin olive oil

12 sage leaves, finely chopped

$\frac{1}{2}$ cup (50 g) pitted black olives, coarsely chopped

1 tablespoon coarse sea salt

SERVES 4–6
PREPARATION 45 min
RISING TIME 2 h
COOKING 1 h
DIFFICULTY level 2

Filled Focaccia

with gorgonzola and bell peppers

Prepare the focaccia dough following the instructions on pages 4–5. • Preheat the oven to 400°F (200°C/gas 6). • Oil an 8 x 12-inch (20 x 30 cm) baking pan. • Bake the bell peppers in the oven until dark and charred all over, 20–30 minutes. • Place the hot bell peppers in a brown paper bag. Close the bag and let rest for 10 minutes. Peel and seed the bell peppers. Rinse well, dry, and slice thinly. • Turn the dough out onto a lightly floured surface and knead for 5 minutes. • Divide the dough into 2 equal portions and press one portion into the prepared pan using your fingers. Prick with a fork. • Cover with the peppers, garlic, and Gorgonzola. Season with salt and pepper and drizzle with 2 tablespoons of oil. • Roll out the remaining dough into a rectangle large enough to cover the pan. Cover the filling with the dough. • Press the cherry tomatoes into the dough at regular intervals. Sprinkle with the oregano and drizzle with the remaining oil. • Bake until the focaccia is golden brown, 25–30 minutes. • Serve hot or at room temperature.

1 lb (500 g) basic focaccia dough (see pages 4–5)
1/4 cup (60 ml) extra-virgin olive oil
1 large red bell pepper (capsicum)
1 large yellow pepper (capsicum)
1 clove garlic, finely sliced
8 oz (250 g) Gorgonzola cheese, sliced
Salt and freshly ground black pepper
12 cherry tomatoes
1 teaspoon dried oregano

Focaccia
with leeks and bacon

Prepare the focaccia dough following the instructions on pages 4–5. Gradually work 2 tablespoons of the oil into the dough as you knead. Let rise in a warm place until doubled in volume, about 2 hours. • Turn the dough out onto a lightly floured work surface and knead for 5 minutes. • Press the dough into an oiled 8 x 12-inch (20 x 30-cm) baking pan using your fingers. Cover and let rise for 30 minutes. • Preheat the oven to 350°F (180°C/gas 4). • Heat 2 tablespoons of the oil in a large frying pan over medium heat. Add the leeks and sauté for 3–4 minutes. Add the stock and simmer until tender, about 5 minutes. • Sauté the bacon over medium heat until lightly browned. • Stir the bacon and cheeses into the leeks. Season with salt. Beat the egg yolk, milk, and thyme in a small bowl. • Brush the focaccia with the remaining oil. Spread with the leek mixture. Drizzle with the egg. • Bake until golden brown, about 30 minutes. • Serve hot or at room temperature.

1 lb (500 g) basic focaccia dough (see pages 4–5)
1/2 cup (125 ml) extra-virgin olive oil
5 medium leeks, finely sliced
1/4 cup (60 ml) vegetable stock
4 oz (125 g) bacon, chopped
1 cup (125 g) freshly grated Gruyère
2 tablespoons freshly grated Parmesan
Salt
1 large egg yolk
1/4 cup (60 ml) milk
1 tablespoon finely chopped thyme

SERVES 4–6
PREPARATION 35 min
RISING TIME 2 h 30 min
COOKING 20–25 min
DIFFICULTY level 2

Focaccia
with rosemary

Prepare the focaccia dough following the instructions on pages 4–5.
• Preheat the oven to 450°F (250°C/gas 8). • Oil a 12-inch (30-cm) pizza or quiche pan. • Turn the dough out onto a lightly floured work surface and knead for 5 minutes. • Press the dough into the prepared pan using your fingers. • Sprinkle with the coarse sea salt and rosemary. Drizzle with the remaining oil. • Bake until golden brown, 20–25 minutes. • Serve hot or at room temperature.

1 lb (500 g) basic focaccia dough (see pages 4–5)
2 tablespoons extra-virgin olive oil
1 tablespoon coarse sea salt
2 tablespoons finely chopped rosemary

SERVES 4–6
PREPARATION 35 min
RISING TIME 2 h
COOKING 1 h
DIFFICULTY level 3

Baby Focaccias

with olives and pine nuts

Prepare the focaccia dough following the instructions on pages 4–5.
• Preheat the oven to 425°F (220°C/gas 7). • Bake the bell peppers
in the oven until dark and charred all over, 20–30 minutes. • Place
the hot bell peppers in a brown paper bag. Close the bag and let rest
for 10 minutes. Peel and seed the bell peppers. Rinse well, dry, and
slice thinly. • Oil two baking sheets. • Turn the dough out onto a
lightly floured work surface and knead for 5 minutes, adding the
olive paste as you work. • Divide the dough into 16 equal portions
and press into disks about ½ inch (1 cm) thick. Place on the
prepared baking sheets. • Top each disk with some of the peppers,
olives, and pine nuts. Season with salt and pepper. Drizzle with the
remaining oil. • Bake until golden brown, about 15 minutes. • Serve
hot or at room temperature.

1 lb (500 g) basic focaccia dough
   (see pages 4–5)
2 tablespoons extra-virgin olive oil
1 small green bell pepper (capsicum)
1 small yellow bell pepper (capsicum)
1 small red bell pepper (capsicum)
3 tablespoons black olive paste
16 black olives, pitted and coarsely
   chopped
2 tablespoons pine nuts
Salt and freshly ground black pepper

Potato Focaccia
filled with tuna and cheese

Cook the potatoes in a large pot of salted boiling water until tender, 10–15 minutes. Drain well. Place in a large bowl and mash until smooth. • Oil a 9-inch (23-cm) square baking dish. • Dissolve the yeast in the milk. • Add the yeast mixture to the potatoes together with the Parmesan, flour, and salt. Mix well. • Spread half the mixture in the prepared baking dish. Cover with a layer of sliced cheese. Top with the tomatoes and tuna. Cover with the remaining dough. Sprinkle with bread crumbs. Let rise for 1 hour. • Preheat the oven to 350°F (180°C/gas 4). • Bake until golden brown, about 30 minutes. • Serve hot.

- 1 lb (500 g) potatoes, peeled and cut into chunks
- ½ oz (15 g) fresh yeast or 1 (¼-oz/7-g) package active dry yeast
- ⅓ cup (90 ml) lukewarm milk
- 1 cup (125 g) freshly grated Parmesan cheese
- ⅓ cup (50 g) all-purpose (plain) flour
- Salt
- 3 oz (90 g) cheese slices
- 1 cup (250 ml) canned tomatoes, chopped
- 6 oz (180 g) canned tuna, drained and broken into small pieces
- 2 tablespoons fine dry bread crumbs

44

Cheese Focaccia
with salami

Prepare the focaccia dough following the instructions on pages 4–5. • Preheat the oven to 400°F (200°C/gas 6). • Oil an 8 x 12-inch (20 x 30-cm) baking dish. • Turn the dough out onto a lightly floured work surface and knead for 5 minutes. • Press the dough into the prepared pan using your fingers. • Mix together the ricotta, eggs, parsley, salami, mozzarella, Parmesan, salt, and pepper in a medium bowl. • Spread this mixture over the focaccia. Drizzle with the oil. • Bake until golden brown, 20–25 minutes. • Serve hot or at room temperature.

1 lb (500 g) basic focaccia dough (see pages 4–5)
2 tablespoons extra-virgin olive oil
1 cup (250 g) ricotta cheese, drained
2 large eggs, lightly beaten
2 tablespoons finely chopped parsley
2 oz (60 g) salami, cut into small cubes
2 oz (60 g) fresh mozzarella cheese, cut into small cubes
4 tablespoons freshly grated Parmesan
Salt and freshly ground black pepper

SERVES 4–6
PREPARATION 30 min
RISING TIME 2 h 30 min
COOKING 30 min
DIFFICULTY level 2

Baby Focaccias

with cream cheese and prosciutto

Use the first seven ingredients to prepare the focaccia dough following the instructions on pages 4–5. Let rise in a warm place until doubled in volume, about 2 hours. • Turn out onto a lightly floured work surface and knead for 5 minutes. • Preheat the oven to 400°F (200°C/gas 6). • Cover 2 baking sheets with waxed paper. • Roll out the dough on a lightly floured work surface until ¼ inch (5 mm) thick. Cut into 2-inch (5-cm) disks using a cookie cutter. • Arrange the disks on the prepared baking sheets. • Bake until golden brown, about 15 minutes. • Remove from the oven and let cool. • Beat the Gorgonzola, cream, and walnuts in a bowl until well mixed. • Beat the cream cheese, chives, green peppercorns, pine nuts, and salt in another bowl. • Spread a quarter of the disks with the Gorgonzola mixture and top with a slice of prosciutto. Spread a quarter of the disks with the cream cheese mixture and top with a slice of prosciutto. • Cover with the remaining disks. • Serve at once.

Dough
1 oz (30 g) fresh yeast or 2 (¼-oz/7-g) packages active dry yeast
1 tablespoon sugar
⅓ cup (90 ml) lukewarm milk
1 cup (150 g) whole-wheat (wholemeal) flour
1 cup (150 g) all-purpose (plain) flour
⅓ cup (50 g) cornstarch (cornflour)
Salt
Fillings
5 oz (150 g) Gorgonzola
⅓ cup (90 ml) heavy (double) cream
¾ cup (90 g) walnuts, coarsely chopped
5 oz (150 g) cream cheese
1 tablespoon finely chopped chives
2 teaspoons green peppercorns preserved in brine, drained
⅓ cup (60 g) pine nuts
5 oz (150 g) sliced prosciutto (Parma ham), cut in small squares

SERVES 4–6

PREPARATION 30 min

RISING TIME 2 h

COOKING 30–35 min

DIFFICULTY level 2

Filled Focaccia

with zucchini and basmati rice

Prepare the focaccia dough following the instructions on pages 4–5. Gradually work 1 tablespoon of the oil into the dough as you knead. Let rise in a warm place until doubled in volume, about 2 hours. • Heat 3 tablespoons of the remaining oil in a large frying pan over medium heat. Add the zucchini and garlic and sauté until tender, 7–10 minutes. Season with salt and remove from the heat. • Cook the rice in a large pot of salted boiling water until tender, 12–15 minutes. • Drain well and add to the zucchini mixture. Mix well and let cool slightly. • Add the egg and coriander. Mix well. • Preheat the oven to 400°F (200°C/gas 6) • Oil a baking sheet. • Turn the dough out onto a lightly floured work surface and knead for 5 minutes. • Roll the dough out into a disk about 15 inches (40 cm). Place on the prepared baking sheet. • Place the zucchini mixture in the center of the disk and pull the edges of the dough over the top • Brush with the remaining oil and sprinkle with the sesame seeds. • Bake until golden brown, 30–35 minutes. • Serve hot.

1 lb (500 g) basic focaccia dough (see pages 4–5)

1/4 cup (60 ml) extra-virgin olive oil

4 medium zucchini (courgettes), coarsely grated

1 clove garlic, finely chopped

1/2 cup (100 g) basmati rice

1 large egg, lightly beaten

2 tablespoons finely chopped cilantro (coriander)

2 tablespoons sesame seeds

SERVES 4–6
PREPARATION 50 min
RISING TIME 2 h
COOKING 1 h
DIFFICULTY level 3

Focaccia

with mozzarella and bell peppers

Prepare the focaccia dough following the instructions on pages 4–5. • Preheat the oven to 400°F (200°C/gas 6). • Oil an 8 x 12-inch (20 x 30-cm) baking pan. • Bake the bell peppers in the oven until dark and charred all over, 20–30 minutes. • Place the hot bell peppers in a brown paper bag. Close the bag and let rest for 10 minutes. Peel and seed the bell peppers. Rinse well, dry, and slice thinly. • Toast the pistachios and bread crumbs in a large frying pan over medium heat until lightly browned, 3–4 minutes. • Add 2 tablespoons of the remaining oil, the garlic, marjoram, and orange zest. Mix well and sauté until the garlic is pale gold, about 3 minutes. Remove from the heat. • Turn the dough out onto a lightly floured work surface and knead for 5 minutes. • Press the dough into the prepared pan using your fingers. Prick all over with a fork. • Sprinkle with the pistachio mixture. Top with the peppers and mozzarella. Season with salt and pepper. • Bake until the focaccia is golden brown, 30–35 minutes. • Serve hot or at room temperature.

1 lb (500 g) basic focaccia dough (see pages 4–5)

3 tablespoons extra-virgin olive oil

1 large red bell pepper (capsicum)

1 large yellow bell pepper (capsicum)

²/₃ cup (60 g) chopped pistachios

1 cup (70 g) fresh bread crumbs

1 clove garlic, finely sliced

2 tablespoons finely chopped marjoram

Grated zest of 1 orange

5 oz (150 g) fresh mozzarella cheese, drained and sliced

Salt and freshly ground black pepper

SERVES 4–6
PREPARATION 35 min
RISING TIME 3 h
COOKING 35 min
DIFFICULTY level 1

Focaccia
with prosciutto

Prepare the focaccia dough following the instructions on pages 4–5. Work the prosciutto into the dough as you knead. Let rise in a warm place until doubled in volume, about 2 hours. • Oil a baking sheet. • Roll out the dough on a lightly floured work surface to ⅔ inch (1.5 cm) thick. • Transfer to the prepared baking sheet. Brush with the beaten egg. • Let rise for 1 hour. • Preheat the oven to 400°F (200°C/gas 6). • Bake the focaccia until risen and golden brown, 30–35 minutes. • Serve hot or at room temperature.

1 lb (500 g) basic focaccia dough (see pages 4–5)
4 oz (125 g) sliced prosciutto (Parma ham), cut small pieces
1 small egg, lightly beaten

SERVES 4–6
PREPARATION 35 min
RISING TIME 1 h 30 min
COOKING 15–20 min
DIFFICULTY level 1

Breadsticks
with oregano

Prepare the focaccia dough following the instructions on pages 4–5. Gradually work the lard, 1 tablespoon of the oil, and oregano into the dough as you knead. Let rise in a warm place for 1 hour. • Cover a baking sheet with waxed paper. • Roll out the dough on the waxed paper to ¼ inch (5 mm) thick. Cut into ⅔-inch (2-cm) strips using a fluted pastry wheel. • Space the strips on the baking sheet leaving 1 inch (3 cm) between them. • Brush with the remaining oil. Let rise for 30 minutes. • Preheat the oven to 350°F (180°C/gas 4). • Bake until crisp and golden brown, 15–20 minutes. • Serve hot or at room temperature.

1 lb (500 g) basic focaccia dough (see pages 4–5)

2 oz (60 g) lard, melted

¼ cup (60 ml) extra-virgin olive oil

3 tablespoons finely chopped oregano

SERVES 4–6
PREPARATION 35 min
RISING TIME 1 h 30 min
COOKING 25 min
DIFFICULTY level 1

Focaccia

with tomatoes and pecorino

Prepare the focaccia dough following the instructions on pages 4–5.
• Slice the tomatoes and place in a colander. Sprinkle with salt and let drain for 10 minutes. • Preheat the oven to 450°F (250°C/gas 8). • Oil a baking sheet. • Roll out the dough on a lightly floured work surface into a 12-inch (30-cm) disk. • Transfer the dough to the prepared baking sheet. Dimple the surface with your fingertips. • Bake until pale golden brown, about 20 minutes. • Remove from the oven and cover with the tomatoes and Mozzarella. Season with salt and pepper. Sprinkle with oregano and basil and drizzle with the oil. • Bake for 5 minutes more. • Sprinkle with the Pecorino and serve hot or at room temperature.

1 lb (500 g) basic focaccia dough (see pages 4–5)
2 tablespoons extra-virgin olive oil
10–12 cherry tomatoes
Salt and freshly ground black pepper
8 oz (250 g) mozzarella cheese, thinly sliced
½ teaspoon dried oregano
8 leaves fresh basil, torn
½ cup (60 g) aged Pecorino cheese, thinly sliced

SERVES 4–6
PREPARATION 30 min
RISING TIME 2 h 30 min
COOKING 15–20 min
DIFFICULTY level 1

Focaccia
with prosciutto and parmesan

Prepare the focaccia dough following the instructions on pages 4–5. Let rise in a warm place until doubled in volume, about 2 hours. • Oil a 12-inch (30-cm) pizza or quiche pan. • Press dough into the pan using your fingers.. • Let rise for 30 minutes. • Preheat the oven to 400°F (200°C/gas 6). • Bake until golden brown, 15–20 minutes. • Remove from the oven and top with the prosciutto, arugula, Parmesan, and tomatoes. • Cut into wedges and serve hot.

1 lb (500 g) basic focaccia dough (see pages 4–5)

4 oz (125 g) sliced prosciutto (Parma ham)

4 oz (125 g) arugula (rocket), coarsely chopped

3 oz (90 g) Parmesan cheese, cut into flakes

8–10 cherry tomatoes, halved

Quick Focaccia
with stracchino and arugula

Sift the flour and 1 teaspoon of salt into a large bowl. Add 4 tablespoons of oil and enough water to make a soft dough. • Knead on a lightly floured work surface until smooth and elastic, 5–10 minutes. • Cover and let rest for 20 minutes. • Preheat the oven to 425°F (220°C/gas 7). • Oil a 10-inch (25-cm) baking pan. • Divide the dough into two equal portions. Roll out on a lightly floured work surface into 2 disks the same size as the baking pan. Place 1 disk in the pan. • Spread with the cheese, arugula, oregano, and tomatoes. Cover with the remaining disk of dough. Make cuts in the surface with a knife so that steam can escape during baking. Drizzle with the remaining oil. • Bake until the focaccia is golden brown, 15–20 minutes. • Serve hot or at room temperature.

3 1/3 cups (500 g) all-purpose (plain) flour
Salt
1/3 cup (90 ml) extra-virgin olive oil
2/3 cup (150 ml) lukewarm water
14 oz (400 g) Stracchino or other soft cheese, cut into pieces
4 oz (125 g) arugula (rocket), coarsely chopped
1/2 teaspoon dried oregano
2 large ripe tomatoes, sliced

58

Focaccia
with sweet potatoes

Cook the sweet potatoes in a large pot of boiling water until tender, about 20 minutes. Drain well and mash until smooth, • Dissolve the yeast and sugar in ½ cup (125 ml) of water. • Place the polenta, flour, and salt in a large bowl, Stir in 2 tablespoons of oil, the sweet potatoes, and yeast mixture to make a soft dough. • Knead on a lightly floured work surface until smooth and elastic, 5-10 minutes. • Transfer to an oiled bowl, cover, and let rise for 1 hour. • Turn the dough out onto a lightly floured work surface and knead for 5 minutes. • Oil a 12-inch (30-cm) pizza or quiche pan. • Press the dough into the prepared pan with your fingers. • Drizzle with the remaining oil. Top with the tomatoes, pressing them lightly into the dough. Sprinkle with oregano and season with salt. • Let rise for 30 minutes. Preheat the oven to 425°F (220°C/gas 7). • Bake until golden brown, about 30 minutes. • Serve hot or at room temperature.

3 large sweet potatoes, peeled and cut into chunks
1 oz (30 g) fresh yeast or 2 (¼-oz/7-g) packages active dry yeast
1 teaspoon sugar
1 cup (250 ml) lukewarm water
1⅔ cups (250 g) fine polenta (stoneground cornmeal)
1⅔ cups (250 g) all-purpose (plain) flour
Salt
¼ cup (60 ml) extra-virgin olive oil
5 oz (150 g) cherry tomatoes, halved
1 teaspoon dried oregano

SERVES 4–6

PREPARATION 35 min

RISING TIME 2 h 30 min

COOKING 15 min

DIFFICULTY level 1

Focaccia

with onion and sage

Prepare the focaccia dough following the instructions on pages 4–5. Let rise in a warm place until doubled in volume, about 2 hours. • Spread the onions out on a baking sheet, sprinkle with salt, and let rest for 1 hour. • Rinse and drain well. • Oil a 10 x 15-inch (25 x 38-cm) jelly-roll pan. • Press the dough into the prepared pan using your fingertips. • Top with the onions and sage leaves. Drizzle with the oil and season with salt. • Let rise for 30 minutes. • Preheat the oven to 400°F (200°C/gas 6). • Bake until golden brown, 20–25 minutes. • Serve hot or at room temperature.

1 lb (500 g) basic focaccia dough (see pages 4–5)
3 large white onions, thinly sliced
$\frac{1}{2}$ teaspoon salt
15 leaves fresh sage
$\frac{1}{4}$ cup (60 ml) extra-virgin olive oil

SERVES 4
PREPARATION 25 min
RISING TIME 2 h 30 min
COOKING 25–30 min
DIFFICULTY level 2

Brown Focaccia
with rosemary

Dissolve the yeast in the water. • Sift both flours and the salt into a large bowl. Add the yeast mixture and mix to make a firm dough. • Knead on a lightly floured work surface until smooth and elastic, 5–10 minutes. • Transfer to a floured bowl, cover, and let rise in a warm place until doubled in volume, about 2 hours. • Turn out onto a lightly floured work surface and knead, adding the rosemary as you work, for 5 minutes. • Oil a-12 inch (30-cm) pizza or quiche pan. • Press the dough into the pan using your fingers. Prick with a fork and drizzle with the oil. • Let rise for 30 minutes. • Preheat the oven to 400°F (200°C/gas 6). • Bake until golden brown, 25–30 minutes. • Serve hot or at room temperature.

½ oz (15 g) fresh yeast or 1 (¼-oz/ 7-g) package active dry yeast
⅔ cup (180 ml) lukewarm water
1⅔ cups (250 g) whole-wheat (wholemeal) flour
½ cup (75 g) all-purpose (plain) flour
Salt
1 tablespoon finely chopped rosemary
¼ cup (60 ml) extra-virgin olive oil

Quick Focaccia
with gorgonzola

Put the water in a large saucepan with the butter and a pinch of salt. Bring to a boil over medium heat. Remove from the heat and add the flour. • Mix well to prevent lumps forming and return to low heat. Simmer, stirring constantly, until the mixture comes away from the sides of the saucepan, 3–5 minutes. Remove from the heat and let cool slightly. • Preheat the oven to 350°F (180°C/gas 4). • Oil a 10-inch (23-cm) springform pan. • Add the eggs one at a time to the cooled mixture. Add two-thirds of the Gorgonzola and mix well. • Spoon the mixture into the prepared pan. Top with the remaining cheese. • Bake until risen and golden brown, 25–30 minutes. • Serve hot.

1 1/4 cups (300 ml) water
1/2 cup (125 g) butter, cut into pieces
Salt
1 2/3 cups (250 g) all-purpose (plain) flour
4 large eggs
8 oz (250 g) Gorgonzola, cut into small cubes

Index

Focaccia

was created and produced by McRae Books Srl

Borgo Santa Croce, 8 – Florence (Italy)

info@mcraebooks.com

Publishers: Anne McRae and Marco Nardi

Project Director: Anne McRae

Design: Sara Mathews

Text: Carla Bardi

Editing: Osla Fraser

Photography: Mauro Corsi, Leonardo Pasquinelli, Gianni Petronio, Lorenzo Borri, Stefano Pratesi

Home Economist: Benedetto Rillo

Artbuying: McRae Books

Layouts: Adina Stefania Dragomir

Repro: Fotolito Raf, Florence

ISBN 978-88-89272-92-3

Printed and bound in China